Preschool Prodigies

CHAPTER FIVE

5

By: Robert and Samantha Young

Illustrations: Robert Young with art licensed at FreePik.com

All rights reserved. No part of this publication may be reproduced, stored in a retrieval system, or transmitted by any means without the express permission of Preschool Prodigies and Young Music, LLC.
Published by: Young Music, LLC
ISBN:978-0999219130
Copyright © 2017
Preschool Prodigies and Young Music, LLC
2358 Dutch Neck Road
Smyrna, DE 19977

Prodigies Playground

THIS BOOK BELONGS TO:

_____

Dear families & teachers,

Welcome back to Preschool Prodigies... prepare for Happy Musicing! In this chapter, we'll focus on a peculiar group of musical notes, Mi Sol & La.

Melodies with Mi, Sol and La are used by children across cultures, languages and continents, so much so that some researchers argue that this combination of notes is instinctual.

When children tease "na na na na boo boo" or "nanny nanny, you can't catch me," they're using patterns of Mi, Sol and La. If you know the songs "It's Raining, It's Pouring," "Doggie Doggie, Where's My Bone," or "Lucy Locket," they're all made up of Mi, Sol and La. If you want to learn more about the strange history behind these three notes, visit the Prodigies Blog.

This workbook is a little bit different from the others in that in contains some songs that are not taught with a video lesson. With these extra songs you can practice the musical skill of sight reading, aka, "play the page."

The songs in this book also have an optional (and more advanced) rhythmic component underneath the lyrics. You'll see in Line 3 several numbers and plus signs, which are a short-hand way of notating rhythm.

1. Ack	- a	back	- a	sod	- a	crack	-er
2. (sol)	(sol)	(la)	(la)	(sol)	(sol)	(mi)	(mi)
3. 1	+	2	+	3	+	4	+

In the above example, you would read line 3 as "one and two and three and four and." And with practice, you would aim to sing the line in pitch with the colors/notes/melody.

We call this process of calling out the numbers and their subdivisions "counting out loud" or "marking the rhythm." By singing out the beat numbers (1 2 3 4) and any follow subdivisions (i.e. the "+" pronounced "and"), we can communicate rhythms quickly and with exact placement. While you can play "Ti-Ti Ta" in lots of different places, "1 + 2" has a definite placement.

Try to count through the rhythms with your learners and enjoy the workbook!

Happy Musicing,

- Mr. Rob & the Prodigies Team

Mi Sol La Bell Mat

Use this bell mat when practicing Mi, Sol & La and when playing along with Chapter 5.

- mi — E / 3
- sol — G / 5
- la — A / 6

Preschool Prodigies – Chapter Five Workbook

Chapter 5 🎵 Section 1: Mi Sol La Warm Up 🎵 Lesson Guide

Objective
By the end of this section, students should be able to differentiate between the hand-signs for E, G and A.

Overview
In this section, students use Mi, Sol and La to play a warm up and "Hammer Ring". Students practice hand-signs in this section.

Essential Question
How can a student perform the hand-signs for the notes E, G and A?

Instruction Tips
Hang the poster from this section in your music practice space and reference it often. Try conducting your learner just using this poster.

Materials
- E Bell • G Bell • A Bell
- Yellow Crayon • Teal Crayon
- Purple Crayon
- Mi Sol La Warm Up Video Access
- Workbook pages: 8-17
- Scissors

Table of Contents

Mi, Sol, La Warm Up Song Sheets	8
Hammer Ring	10
Mi, Sol, La Hand-Signs	13
Mi, Sol, La Hand-Signs	15
Hand-Sign Cut-Outs	17

Complementary Activities
Have one student use the hand-sign poster to conduct the class in a "point and response" hand-signing exercise.

Section 5.1 Video Annotations

0:00 Explain to students that this is a warm up with the notes Mi, Sol and La. They should take out their E, G and A bells, but we'll begin by just singing and hand-signing.

2:42 Mr. Rob switches from hand-signs and Solfège names to deskbells and scale degrees.

3:42 Mr. Rob begins a faster call and response pattern. Pause if your learners are having trouble with the pace and go back to the beginning of this section.

Mi Sol La Warm Up
Lesson 5.1

☆☆☆☆☆

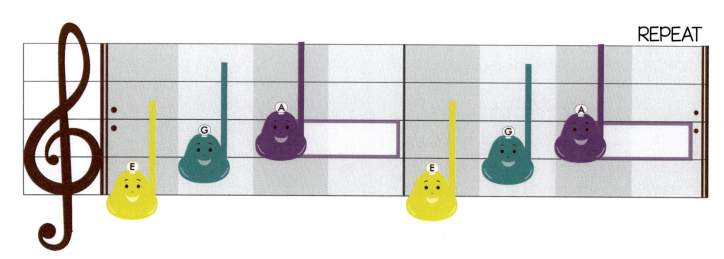

Mi Sol La   Mi Sol La

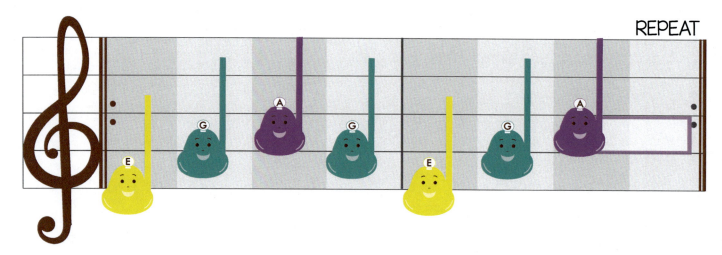

Mi Sol La Sol Mi Sol La

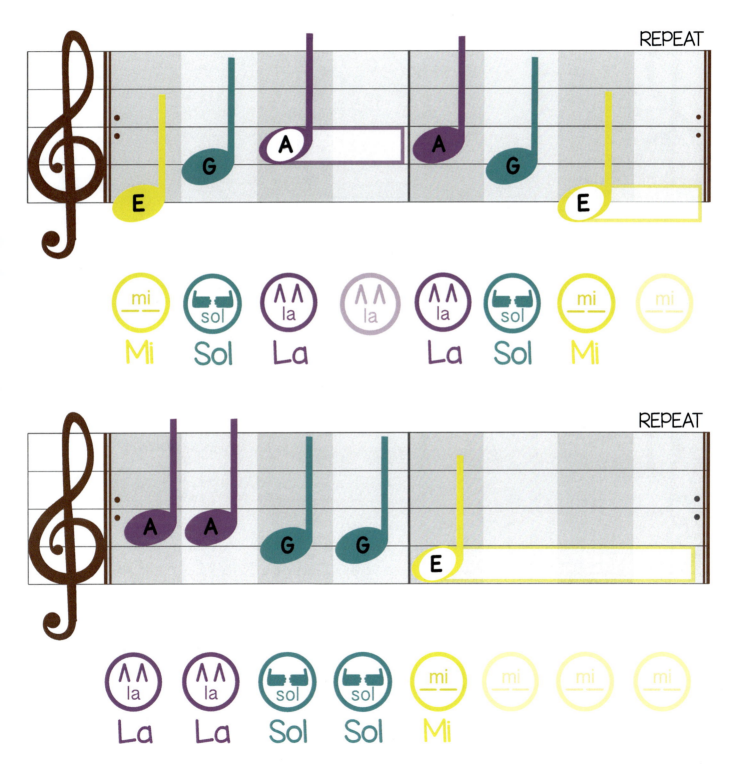

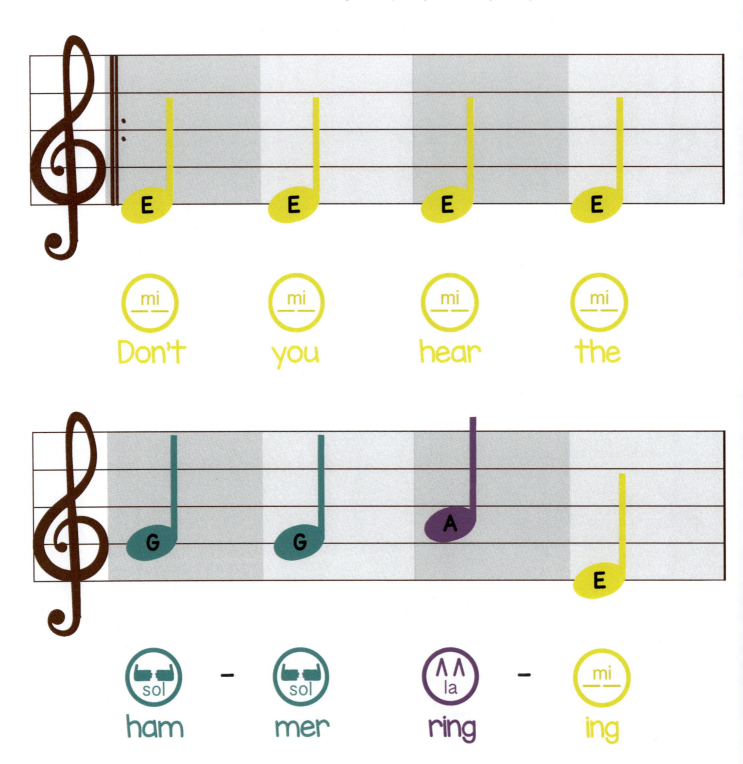

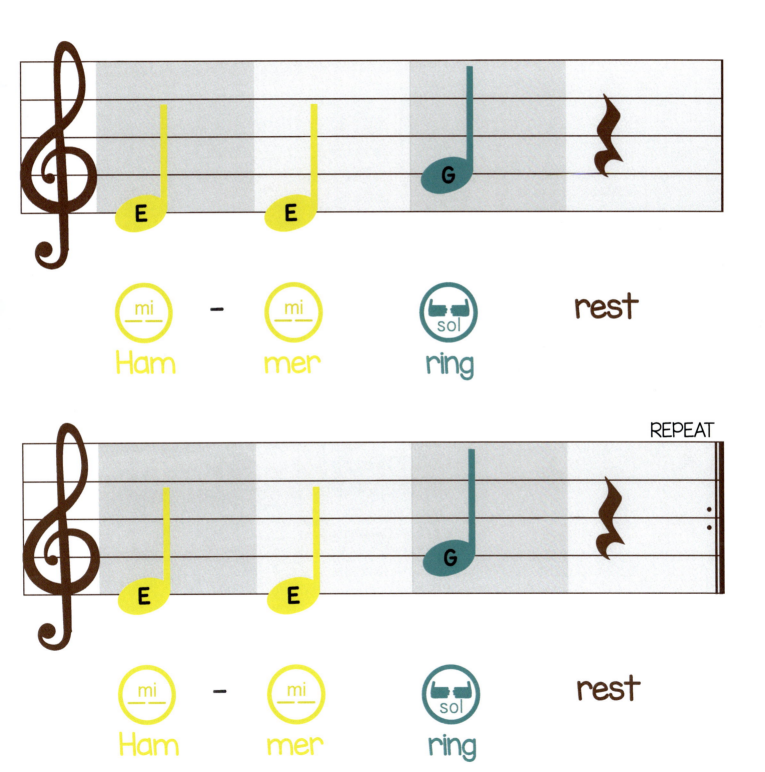

Mi Sol La Hand-Signs
Point and Sign Poster

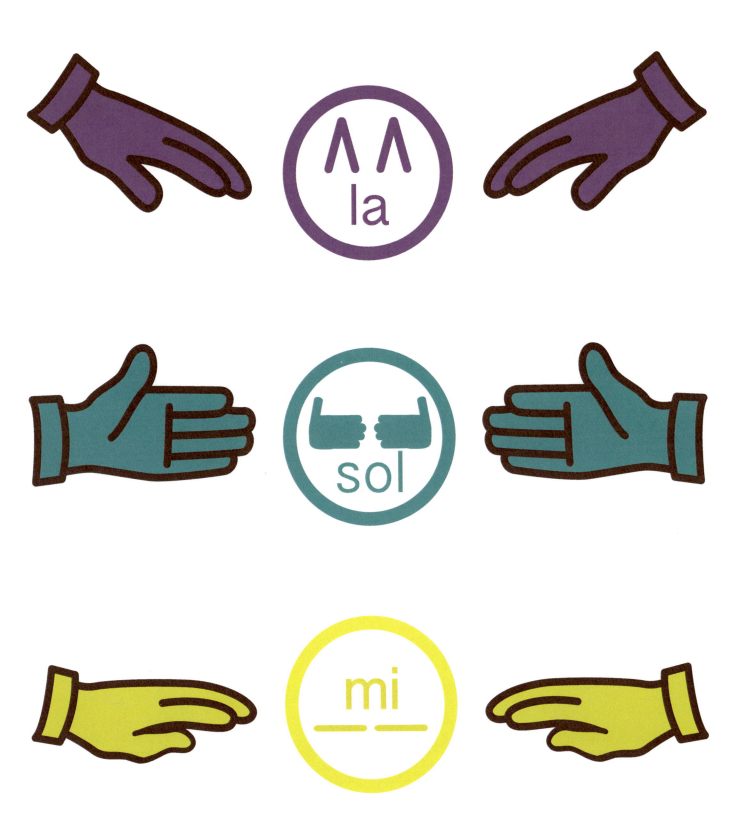

Mi Sol La Hand-Signs

In this chapter, we'll learn and practice the hand-signs for the next three musical notes: Mi, Sol and La. The signs will make it easier for you and your learner to feel the different sensations of each note.

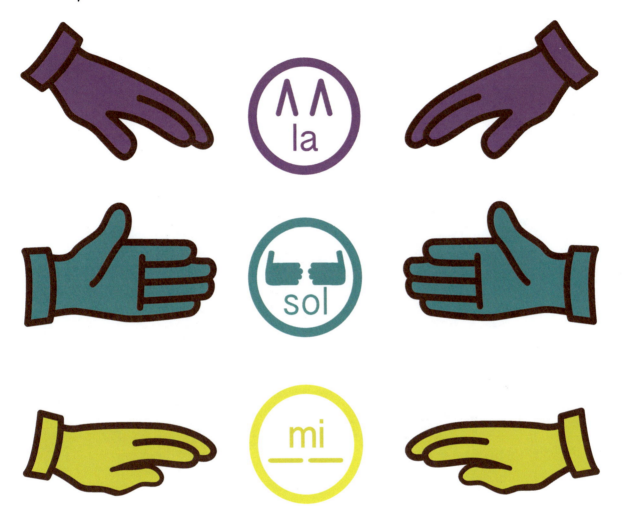

The detailed drawings of the hand-signs are visible here.

In the middle are some of the simplified versions that we use inside the Playground videos.

The simplified signs are easier to write on a board if you're a teacher and easy enough for kids to draw.

For extra practice, try playing a bell (Yellow, Teal or Purple) and then singing the Solfège while making the hand-sign. Have your child sing and sign along, or even have them play a bell and then sing and sign.

Hand-Sign Cut-Outs

Cut out these hand-sign cards. Then arrange them in your own pattern. Then sing and hand-sign your Mi, Sol La melody. You can make a melody with 4, 8 or all 12 cards.

Preschool Prodigies - Chapter Five Workbook

Chapter 5 Section 2: Doggie, Doggie Lesson Guide

Objective
By the end of this section, students should be able to play "Doggie, Doggie" using E, G & A.

Overview
In this section, students use both eighth notes and quarter notes to play Mi, Sol, La songs, then try to identify E, G & A by ear.

Essential Question
How can a student identify E, G and A?

Instruction Tips
Have students take turns being the one who sees the bells in the listening game. That way, each learner gets a chance to both see the bells while quizzing another, and try to guess themselves.

Materials
- E Bell • G Bell • A Bell
- Yellow Crayon • Teal Crayon
- Purple Crayon
- Doggie, Doggie Video Access
- Workbook pages: 20-28

Table of Contents

Doggie Doggie Song Sheets	20
Bounce High, Bounce Low	24
Listen and Color	26
Finish the Pattern	27
Match the Hand-Signs	28

Complementary Activities
Ask your learner to create his or her own Mi, Sol, La pattern and play it for you, then play it back for him or her. Take turns creating a pattern for the other to replicate.

Section 5.2 Video Annotations

0:00 Explain to students that this video will use Mi, Sol and La. They should take out their E, G and A bells, but we'll begin by just singing and hand-signing.

1:04 Students begin singing the bell colors and playing along on the bells.

1:41 Students begin singing note names while playing their bells.

2:15 Students begin singing the lyrics to "Doggie Doggie Where's your Bone?" while playing their bells.

Preschool Prodigies - Chapter Five Workbook

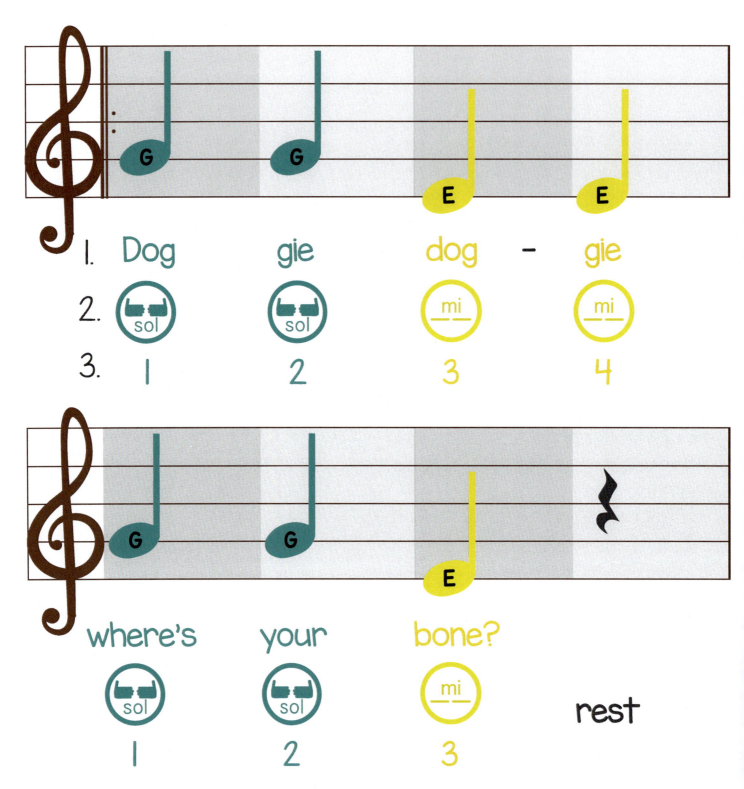

If you're playing the game Doggie Doggie, you can also sing this little ending bit right before the chase part of the game starts!

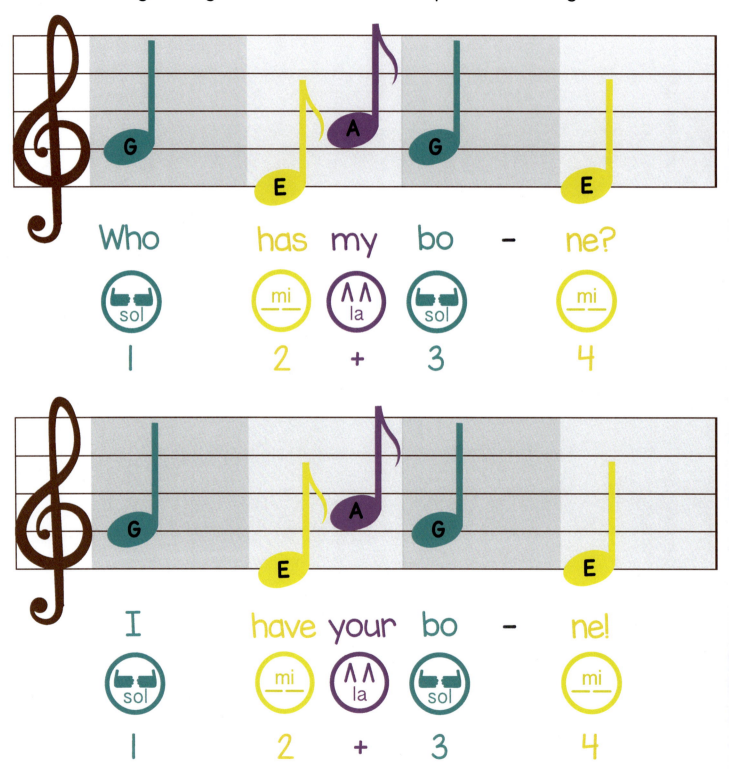

Bounce High, Bounce Low

☆☆☆☆☆

Here's another song you probably don't know, but it's very similar to Doggie Doggie! Try to sing & play it below.

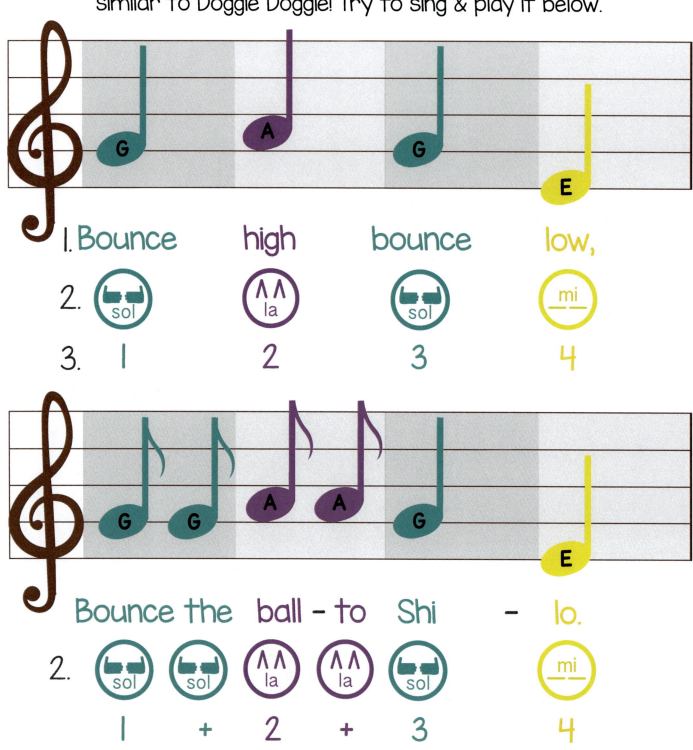

24 Preschool Prodigies - Chapter Five Workbook

Listen and Color

In this activity, Player 1 (teacher) plays the bells while Player 2 (student) listens and tries to color the bell that was played! Do a warm-up round with no coloring and maybe with the bells in sight, but when you're ready to begin, make sure Player 2 cannot see the bells!

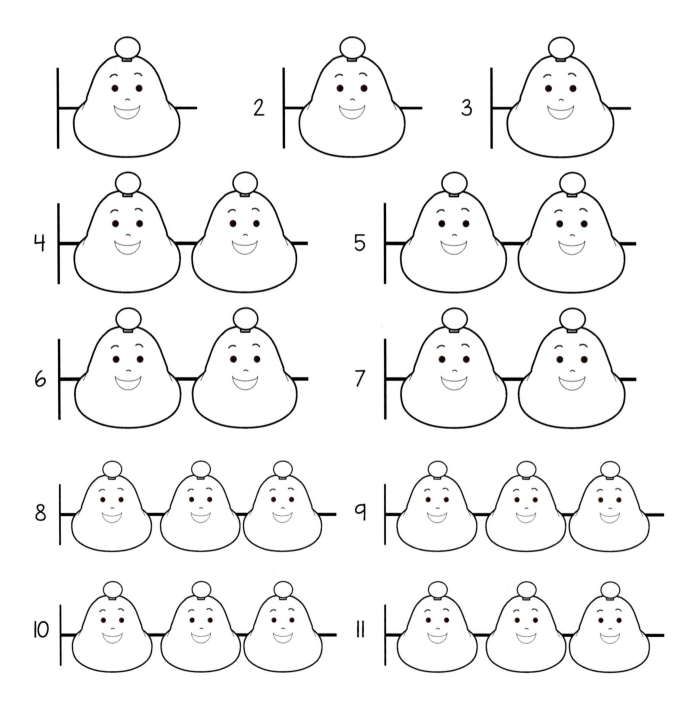

Finish the Pattern

Finish the patterns below. Then practice playing them on your instrument! Try singing the numbers as you play.

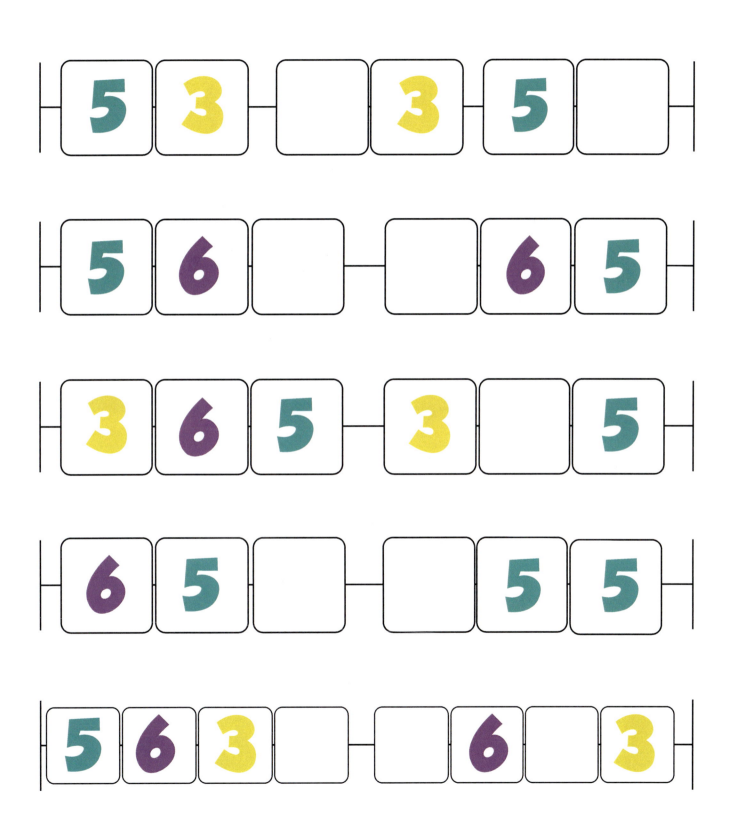

Preschool Prodigies – Chapter Five Workbook

Match the Hand-Signs

Draw a line between each Solfège hand-sign and the correct hand position.

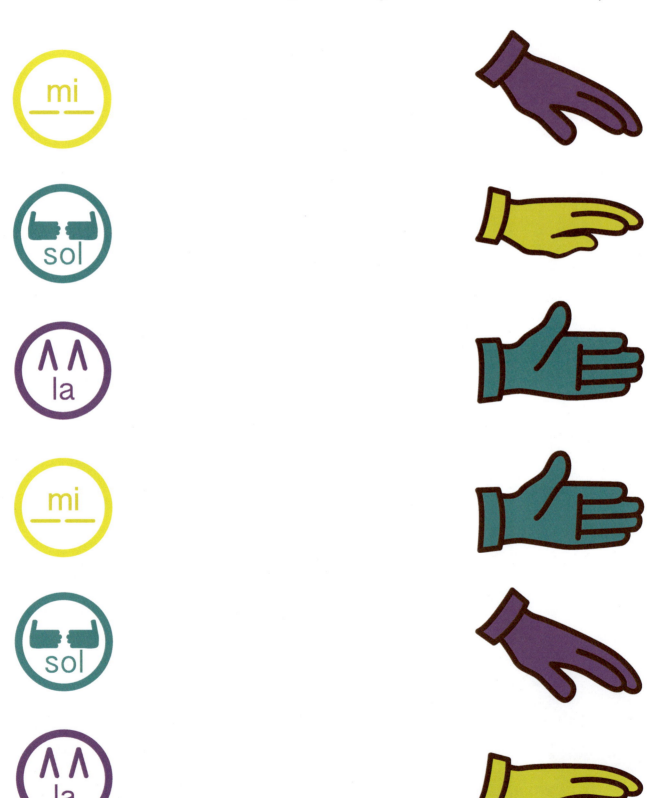

28 Preschool Prodigies - Chapter Five Workbook

Chapter 5 🎵 Section 3: It's Raining, It's Pouring 🌟 Lesson Guide

Objective
By the end of this section, students should be able to play "It's Raining, It's Pouring" with E, G & A.

Overview
In this section, students learn to play "It's Raining, It's Pouring", then make up new lyrics to the song.

Essential Question
How can a student use Mi, Sol and La to play "It's Raining, It's Pouring"?

Instruction Tips
This song can be a little tricky for students. Give them plenty of opportunities to play it, including when they write new lyrics for it.

Materials
- E Bell • G Bell • A Bell
- Yellow Crayon • Teal Crayon
- Purple Crayon
- It's Raining, It's Pouring Video Access
- Workbook pages: 30-36

Table of Contents

It's Raining, It's Pouring Song Sheets	30
Rain Dance	32
E, G & A Coloring	34
Write a Song Using 3, 5 & 6	35
Write New Lyrics	36

Complementary Activities
Ask your learner to think about other things that starter with the letters E, G and A or things that are the colors yellow, purple or teal.

Section 5.3 Video Annotations

0:00 Explain to students that in this video they will continue practice with Mi, Sol and La. They should take out their E, G and A bells, but we'll begin by just singing and hand-signing.

1:16 Pause here and ask students how they did following along with that pace. If necessary, go back to 0:51 and sing and hand-sign once more before moving on.

1:27 Students sing and play along using the bell colors.

2:03 Students sing and play along using the note names.

2:42 Students begin singing the lyrics to "It's Raining, It's Pouring".

It's Raining, It's Pouring
Lesson 5.3
☆☆☆☆☆

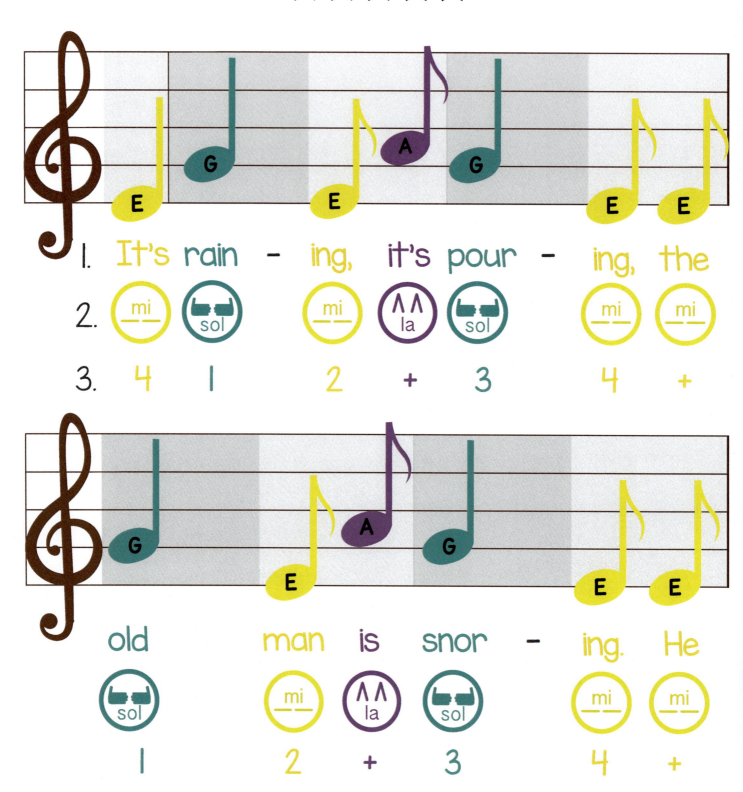

30 Preschool Prodigies - Chapter Five Workbook

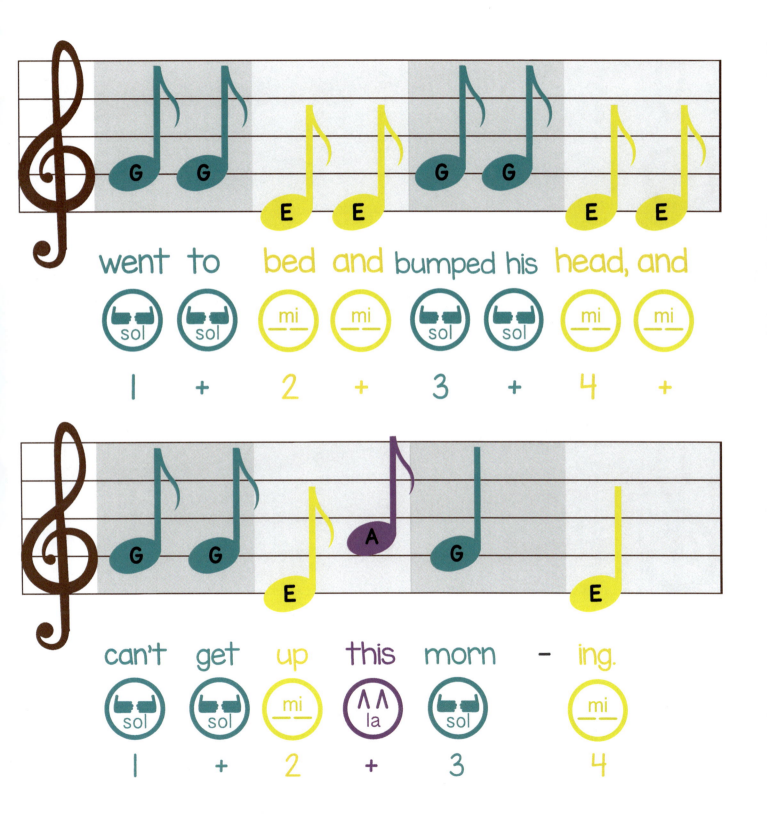

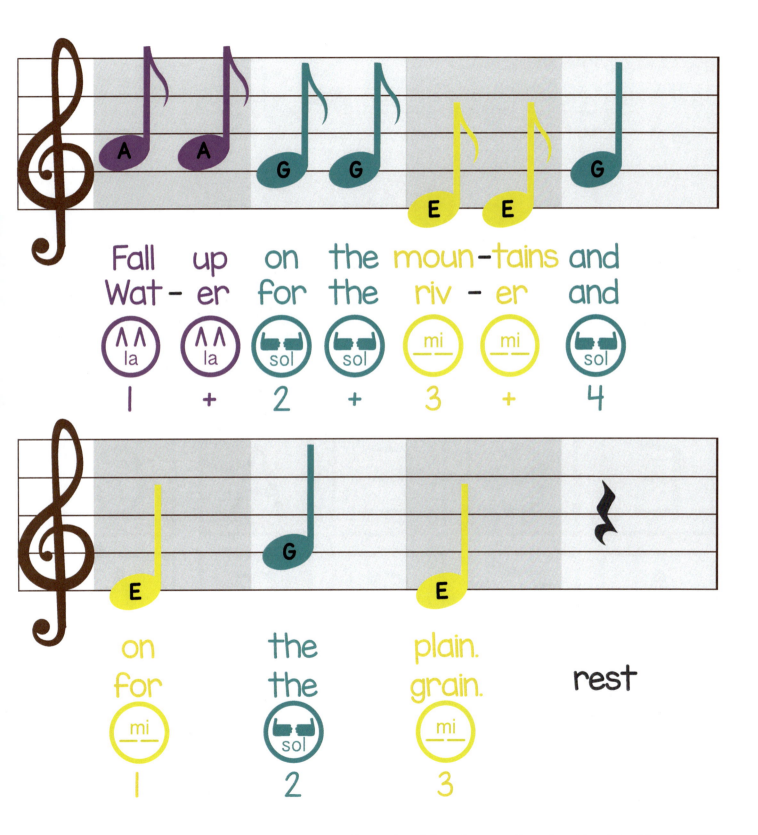

E, G & A Coloring

Play the pattern of notes below with your E, G & A bells. Then sing it with the Mi, Sol & La hand-signs. After that, color in E boxes yellow, G boxes teal & A boxes purple.

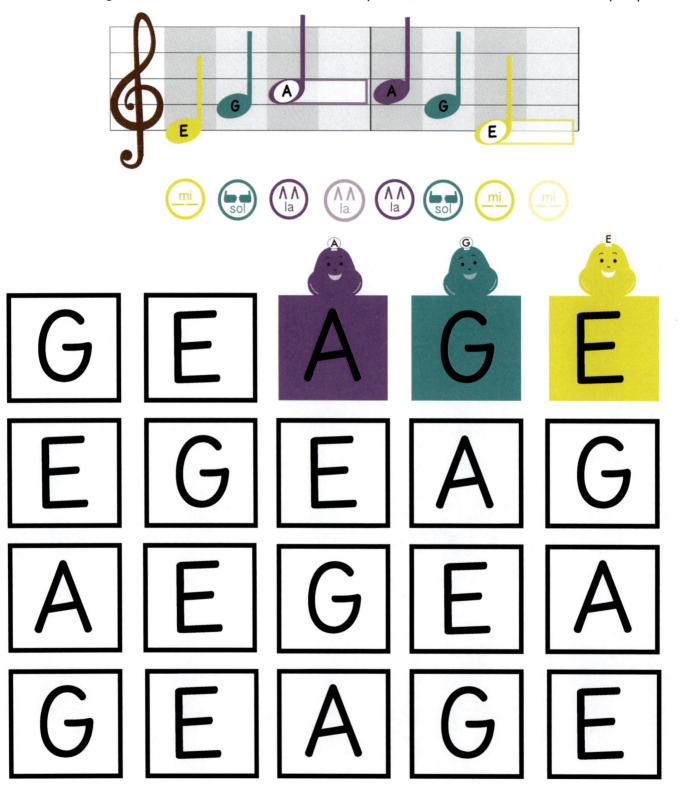

Write a Song Using

Write a song using the numbers and then play it on your bells!
Challenge: Add one word to each box for lyrics!

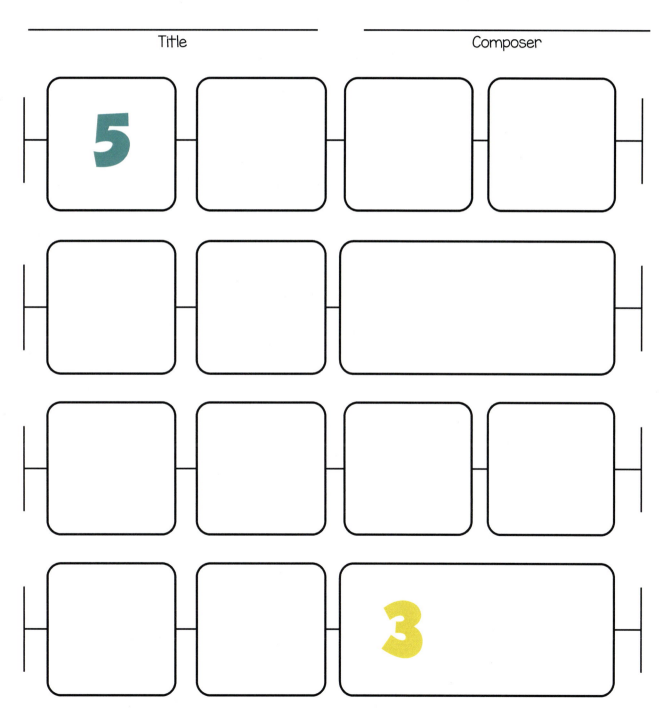

Title   Composer

Preschool Prodigies – Chapter Five Workbook

Write New Lyrics

Write your own words to the tune of It's Raining, It's Pouring!

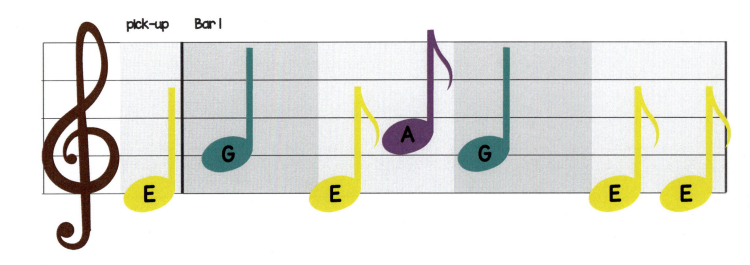

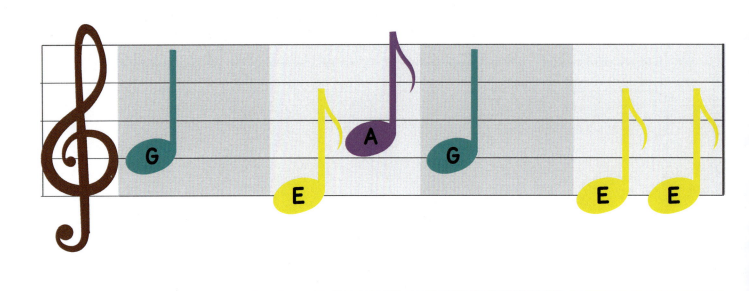

36 Preschool Prodigies – Chapter Five Workbook

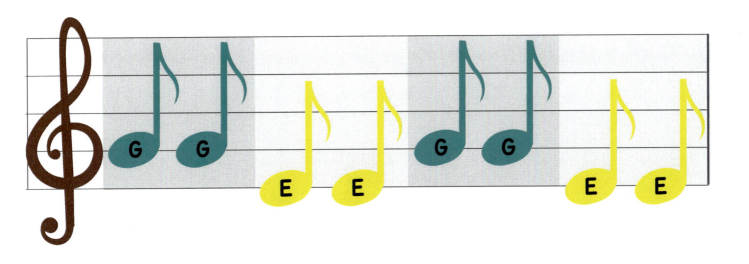
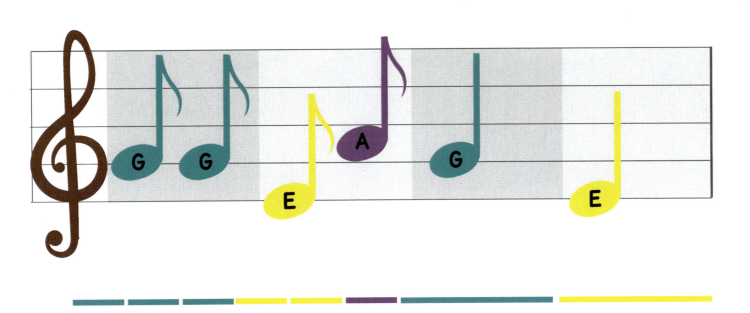

Chapter 5 ♪ Section R: Beet & Avocado ♪ Lesson Guide

Objective
By the end of this section, students should be able to clap, tap or stomp a sixteenth note.

Overview
In this section, students will learn about sixteenth notes and their relationship to other beats.

Essential Question
How is a sixteenth note different from an eighth note or quarter note?

Instruction Tips
Students learn sixteenth notes in this section, which can be very difficult for young students to understand. Take your time to review each word in the Sixteenth & Eighth Notes activity, and pronounce each syllable.

Materials
- Beet & Avocado Video Access
- Workbook pages: 40-50

Table of Contents

Beet & Avocado Song Sheets	40
Rhythm Cards	43
Sixteenth & Eighth Notes	47
Sixteenth Notes	49
Beat Math	50

Complementary Activities
Make up your own rhythm pattern as a class. Have student volunteers suggest notes and the teacher records it on the board. Then, everyone claps or stomps together.

Section 5.R Video Annotations

0:22 Pause here and have students practice saying "avocado".

1:48 Pause here and have students practice saying "tika tika" to represent a sixteenth note.

2:03 Students sing along using numbers to count the beats.

3:35 Mr. Rob explains sixteenth notes & using syllables to represent beats.

Beet & Avocado
Lesson 5.R
☆☆☆☆☆

Clap, tap or stomp along while you sing with the sheet music below after you've watched the Beet & Avocado video in section 5.R.

CHORUS 1

Sweet Beets, we've got some!
If you want some Sweet Beets, we've got 'em.
If you want Sweet Beets, we've got some,
If you want some Sweet Beets, we've got 'em.

VERSE 1

BEET   BEET   AVOCADO   BEET   AVOCADO   AVOCADO   BEET   BEET

AVOCADO   BEET   AVOCADO   BEET   AVOCADO   AVOCADO   AVOCADO   BEET

CHORUS 2

Sweet Beets, we've got some!
If you want some Sweet Beets, we've got 'em.
If you want Sweet Beets, we've got some,
If you want some Sweet Beets, we've got 'em.

VERSE 2

TA   TA   TIKA TIKA TA   TIKA TIKA TIKA TIKA TA   TA

TIKA TIKATA   TIKA TIKA TA   TIKA TIKA TIKA TIKA TA   TA

Preschool Prodigies – Chapter Five Workbook

CHORUS 3

Sweet Beets, we've got some!
If you want some Sweet Beets, we've got 'em.
If you want Sweet Beets, we've got some,
If you want some Sweet Beets, we've got 'em.

VERSE 3

CHORUS 4

Sweet Beets, we've got some!
If you want some Sweet Beets, we've got 'em.
If you want Sweet Beets, we've got some,
If you want some Sweet Beets, we've got 'em.

VERSE 4

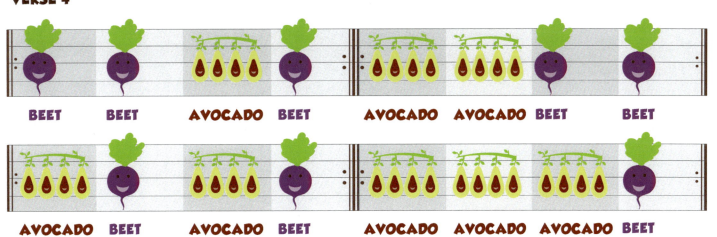

CHORUS 5

Sweet Beets, we've got some!
If you want some Sweet Beets, we've got 'em.
If you want Sweet Beets, we've got some,
If you want some Sweet Beets, we've got 'em.

Rhythm Cards

Cut out each rhythm card below. Then lay them out to create your own pattern. Tap the pattern on your legs! Then mix up the pattern and try again.

Preschool Prodigies - Chapter Five Workbook

Preschool Prodigies - Chapter Five Workbook 45

Sixteenth Notes

Practice clapping and playing along with the sixteenth notes below.

Clap this line 4 times. As you clap, sing the rhythms "One E And Ah Two. Three E And Ah Four." If the clapping seems too fast, try drumming on your legs. Then you can use both hands to play faster rhythms.

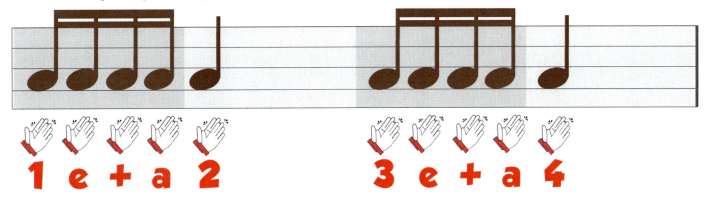

Let's play the same pattern again (four times), but this time with our red bell! Make sure to sing "1 e and a 2,   3 e and a 4"

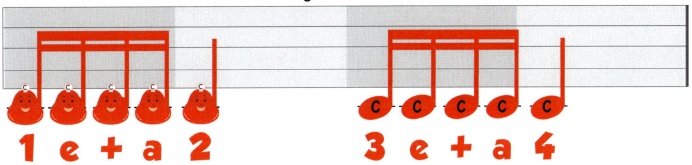

Finally, see if you can play a whole measure of sixteenth notes!! Challenge: Try to play it four times in a row without skipping a beat!

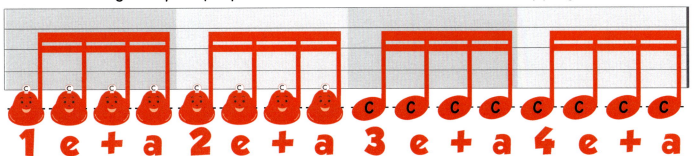

Preschool Prodigies – Chapter Five Workbook

Beat Math

This adding activity is a bit harder, but don't worry – you can do it!
On this page, you'll see how

Chapter 5 🎵 Section 4: Lucy Locket 🎵 Lesson Guide

Objective
By the end of this section, students should be able to play "Lucy Locket" using Mi, Sol and La.

Overview
In this section, student write their own Mi, Sol, La song after playing "Lucy Locket" and "Bobby Shafto".

Essential Question
How can a student use Mi, Sol and La to play "Lucy Locket"?

Instruction Tips
As you complete the activities, play the bells, or encourage your student to play the bells. Each time they use a teal, purple or yellow crayon, encourage them to tap that bell as well.

Materials
- E Bell • G Bell • A Bell
- Yellow Crayon • Teal Crayon
- Purple Crayon
- Lucy Locket Video Access
- Workbook pages: 52-58

Table of Contents

Lucy Locket Song Sheets	52
Bobby Shafto	54
Finish the Pattern	56
Write a Song Using Mi, Sol & La	57
Musical Math	58

Complementary Activities
Ask students to share their original songs with the class. The class could play along in a call and response way with the student-composer leading.

Section 5.4 Video Annotations

0:00 Explain to students that in this video they will continue practice with Mi, Sol and La. They should take out their E, G and A bells, but we'll begin by just singing and hand-signing.

1:28 Students sing and play along using the bell colors.

2:06 Students sing and play along using the note names.

2:42 Students begin singing the lyrics to "Lucy Locket".

Lucy Locket
Lesson 5.4

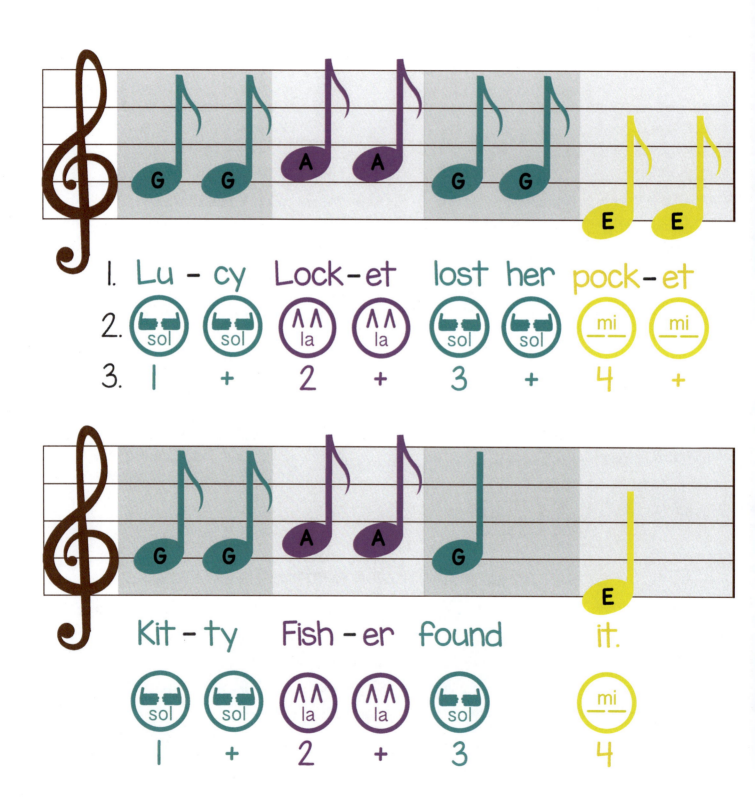

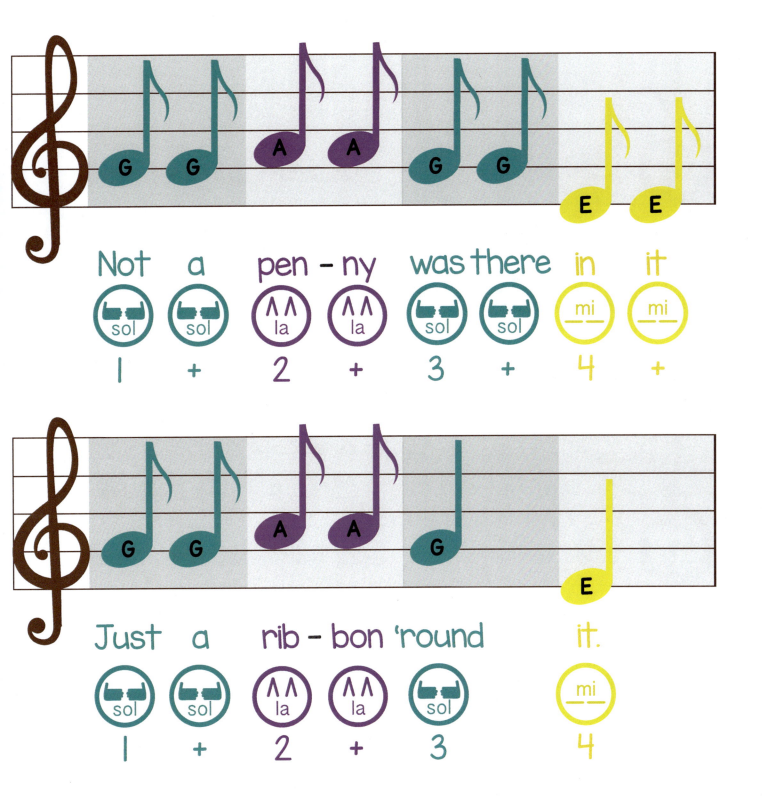

Bobby Shafto

☆☆☆☆☆

Here's another song you probably don't know, but it's very similar to Lucy Locket! Try to sing & play it below.

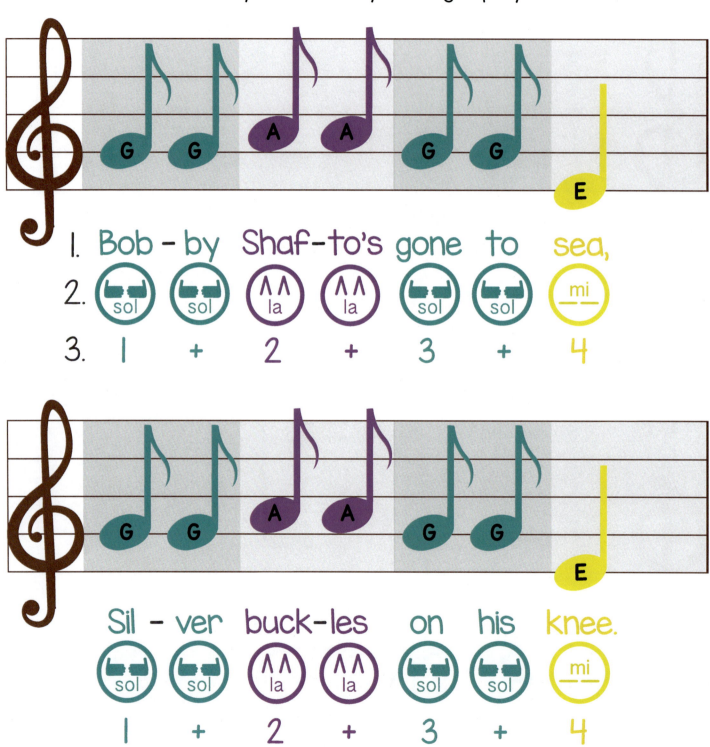

54 Preschool Prodigies – Chapter Five Workbook

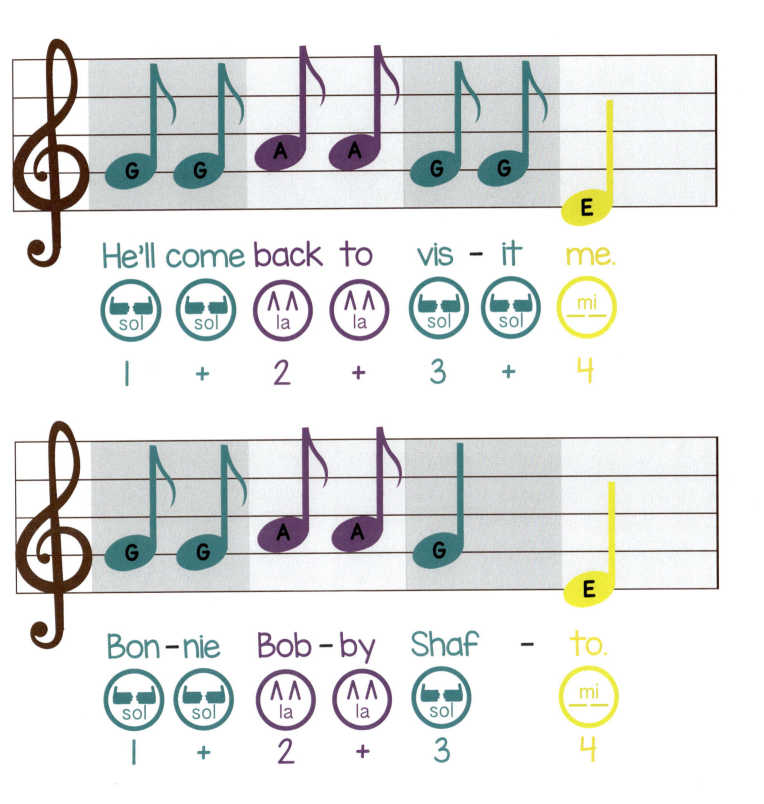

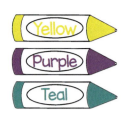

Finish the Pattern

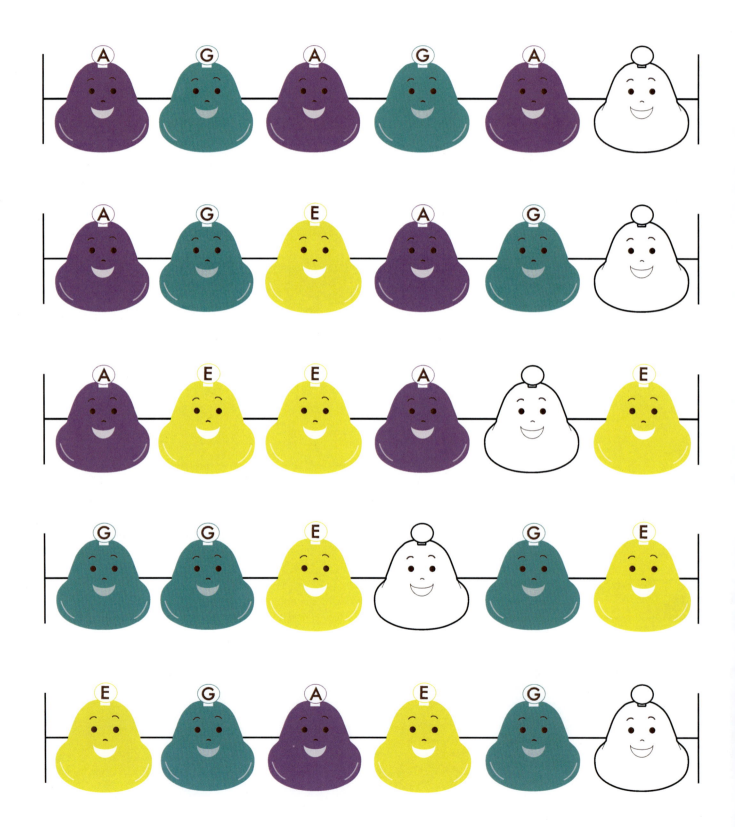

Write a Song Using

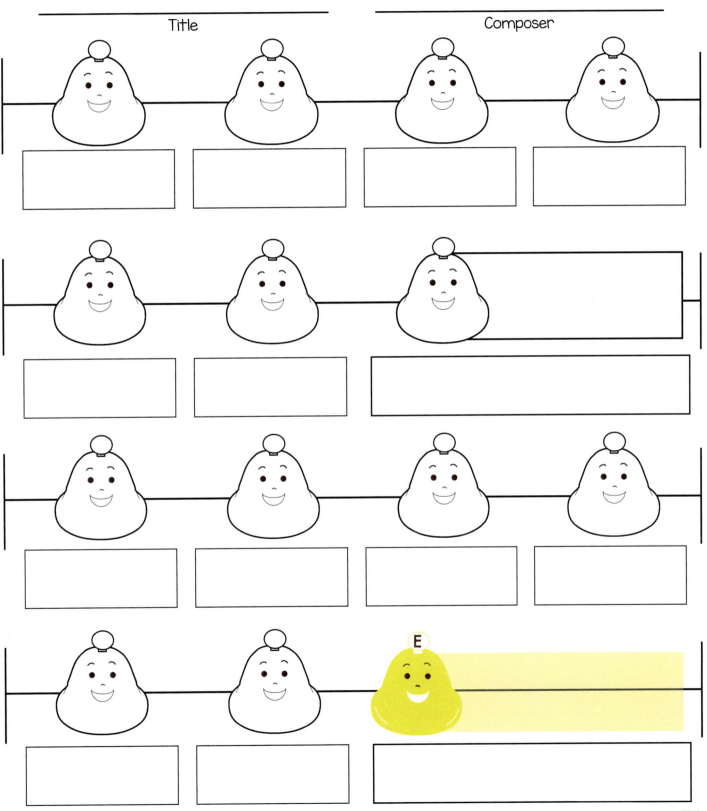

Preschool Prodigies – Chapter Five Workbook

Musical Math

Let's try a simple adding activity with the quarter note and the half note.
The quarter note is one beat. The half note is two beats.
Let's add them up to see how many beats we have!
Hint: Don't worry about the colors on this page. They're just for fun!

♩ = 1   𝅗𝅥 = 2

♩ + ♩ + ♩ = 3

♩ =

♩ + ♩ =

𝅗𝅥 + ♩ + ♩ =

𝅗𝅥 =

♩ + ♩ =

𝅗𝅥 + ♩ =

𝅗𝅥 + 𝅗𝅥 =

♩ + ♩ + ♩ + ♩ + 𝅗𝅥 =

♩ + ♩ + 𝅗𝅥 + ♩ + ♩ + 𝅗𝅥 + =

58   Preschool Prodigies - Chapter Five Workbook

Chapter 5 • Section 5: Acka Backa • Lesson Guide

Objective
By the end of this section, students should be able to play "Acka Backa" using Mi, Sol and La.

Overview
In this section, students continue to practice playing E, G & A, playing songs and learning about Musical Skips.

Essential Question
How can a student use E, G & A to play "Acka Backa"?

Instruction Tips
Use actual stairs or blocks to create a representation of musical skips. Place each bell on the correct step or block to help students further their understanding of musical space.

Materials
- E Bell • G Bell • A Bell
- Yellow Crayon • Teal Crayon
- Purple Crayon
- Acka Backa Video Access
- Workbook pages: 60-66

Table of Contents

Acka Backa Song Sheets	60
Bickle Bockle	62
Musical Skips	64
Musical Skips	65
Mi Sol La Steps, Skips & Same	66

Complementary Activities
Lay down masking tape on the floor of your classroom to create a staff. Call out notes that make up musical skips, and have the kids leap to the line or space where that note lives.

Section 5.5 Video Annotations

0:00 Explain to students that in this video they will continue practice with Mi, Sol and La. They should take out their E, G and A bells, but we'll begin by just singing and hand-signing.

0:35 Pause here and ask students how they did following along with that pace. If necessary, go back to 0:23 and sing and hand-sign once more before moving on.

0:55 Students sing and play along using the scale degrees.

1:54 Students begin singing the lyrics to "Acka Backa".

2:33 Mr. Rob discusses scale degrees and how the numbers can help us understand the relationship between Mi, Sol and La.

Acka Backa
Lesson 5.5

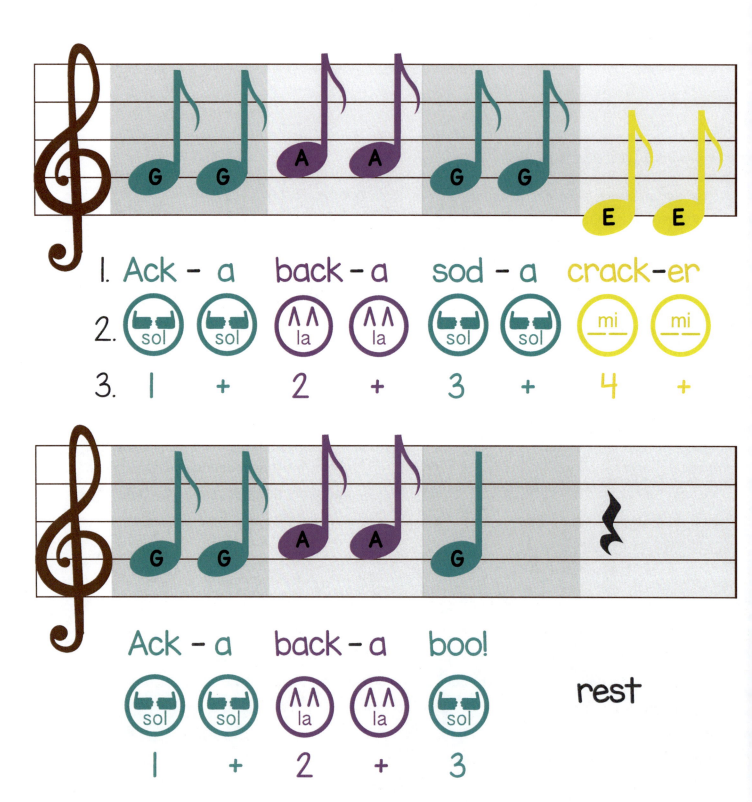

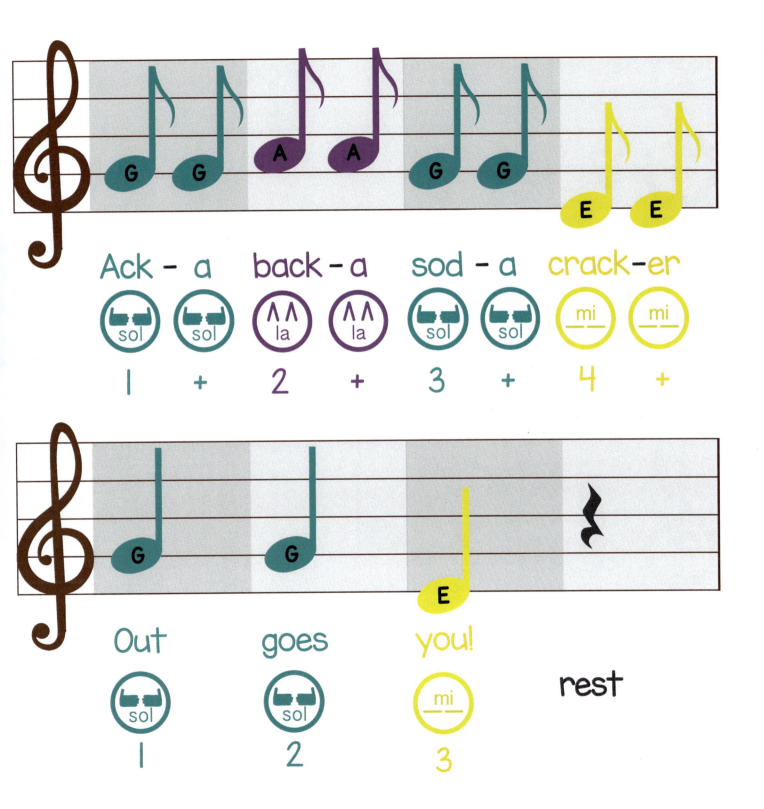

Bickle Bockle

☆☆☆☆☆

Bickle Bockle, like Acka Backa, is a silly song! Even though you may not know it yet, use the sheet music below to figure it out!

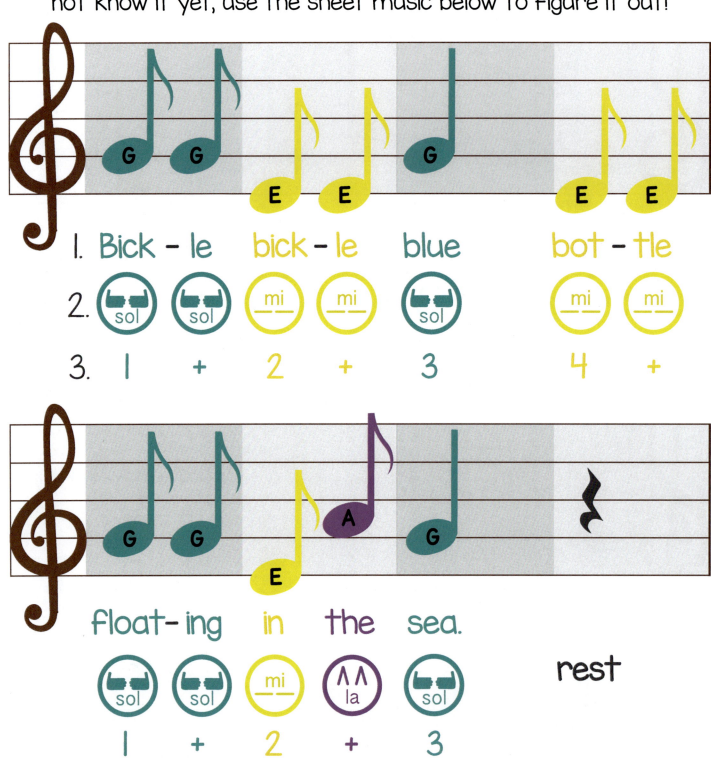

Musical Skips

When we jump over a musical note, we call it a SKIP!

For instance, you can SKIP UP from E to G. This would skip over the note F.

In this Mi, Sol, La book, we skip between E and G a lot.

We also skip between E and A sometimes, which is a bigger kind of skip.

And of course, we step between G and A as well.

Try finding some books and setting up your bells like below. Put 3 books under the E, 5 books under the G, and 6 books under the A.

Then try playing Bickle Bockle one more time!

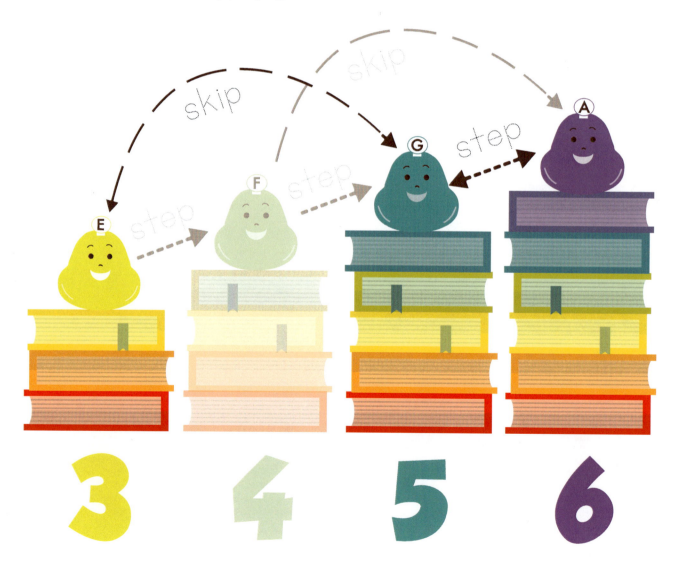

Musical Skips

Can you draw some curved arrows to show all the musical skips below? After that, play your instrument while you sing the numbers of the bells!

Mi Sol La Steps, Skips & Same

On this page, we have steps, skips and stays-the-same (same).
Trace the arrows to practice drawing the different moves.
Then play the bells while singing the scale-degrees (numbers).

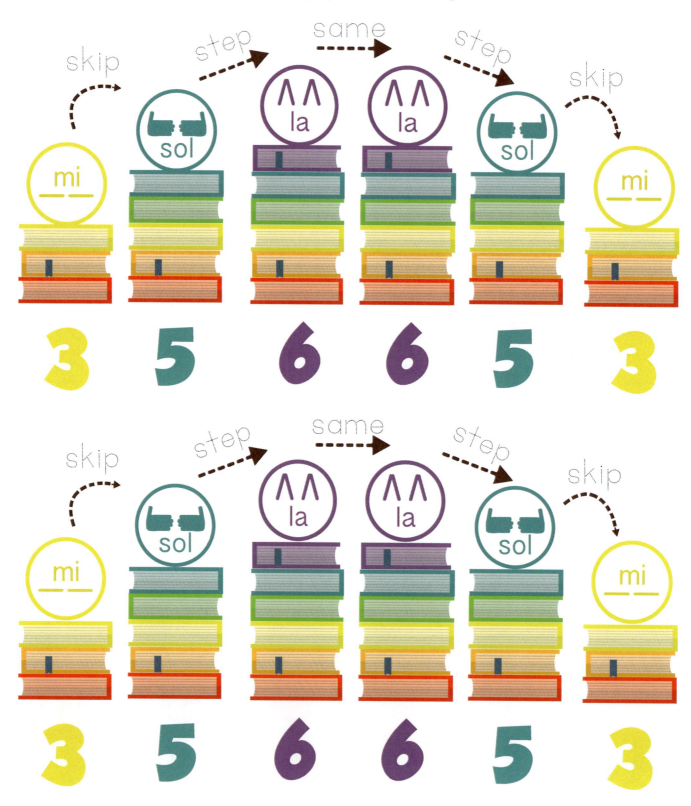

66 Preschool Prodigies - Chapter Five Workbook

Chapter 5 ♪ Section 6: Bye Bye Baby Bunting ♪ Lesson Guide

Objective
By the end of this section, students will be able to play "Bye Bye Baby Bunting".

Overview
In this section, students use Mi, Sol, and La to play "Bye Bye Baby Bunting" and identify wrong notes on the staff..

Essential Question
How can a student use Mi, Sol and La to play "Bye Bye Baby Bunting"?

Instruction Tips
If students are having trouble identifying the correct placement of notes on the staff, let them look back at the song sheets. Alternatively, if students are a little older, you could teach them a mnemonic device that would help them remember the placement, such as: "face in the space" or "every good boy does fine".

Materials
- E Bell • G Bell • A Bell
- Yellow Crayon • Teal Crayon
- Purple Crayon
- Bye Bye Baby Bunting Video Access
- Workbook pages: 68-75
- Scissors

Table of Contents

Bye Bye Baby Bunting Song Sheets	68
Wolf (We are Dancing)	70
Wrong Note	72
Match the Numbers	73
Hand-Sign Memory	75

Complementary Activities
Use the memory cards to write songs and practice sequences, create your own listening game where students use the cards to indicate their guesses, or make up your own game!

Section 5.6 Video Annotations

0:00 Explain to students that in this video they will continue practice with Mi, Sol and La. They should take out their E, G and A bells, but we'll begin by just singing and hand-signing.

0:40 Pause here and ask students how they did following along with that pace. If necessary, go back to 0:30 and sing and hand-sign once more before moving on.

1:05 Students sing and play along using the scale degrees.

2:18 Students begin singing the lyrics to "Bye Bye Baby Bunting".

Bye Bye Baby Bunting
Lesson 5.6

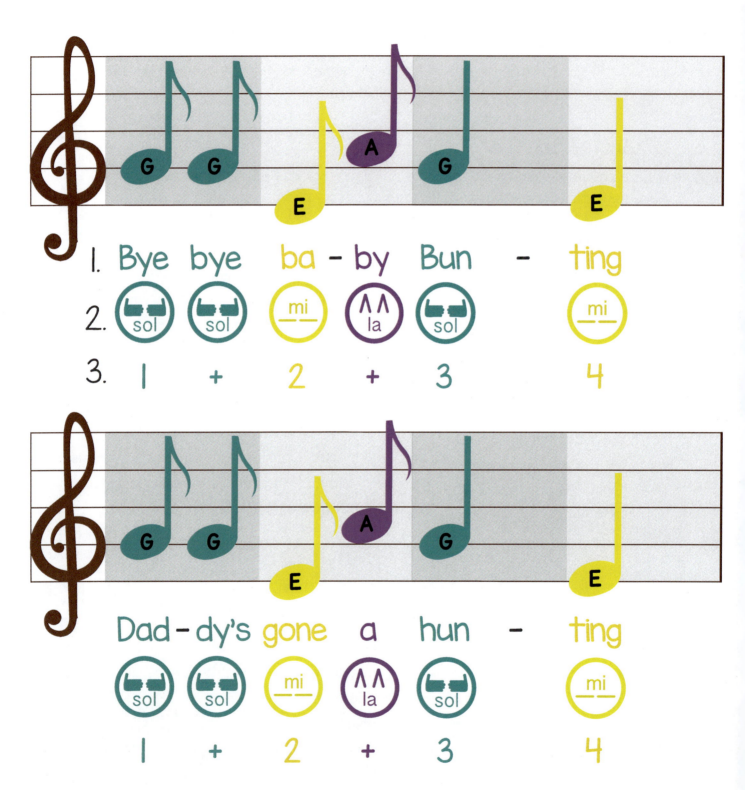

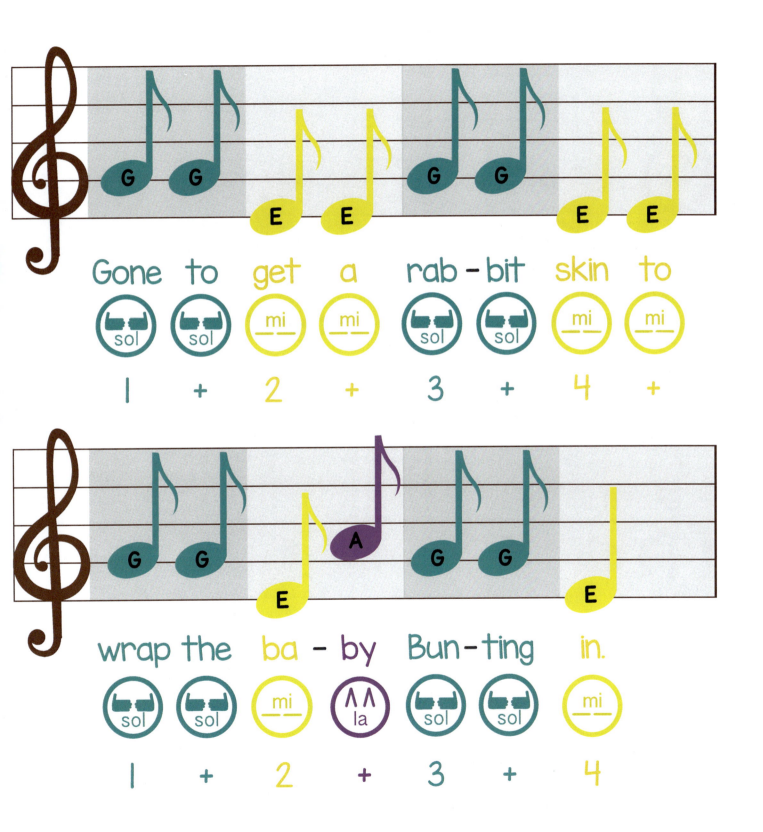

Wolf (We are Dancing)

☆☆☆☆☆

Here's one final Mi, Sol, La song. Try playing this song 3 or 4 times, and then see if you can play it without looking at the music.

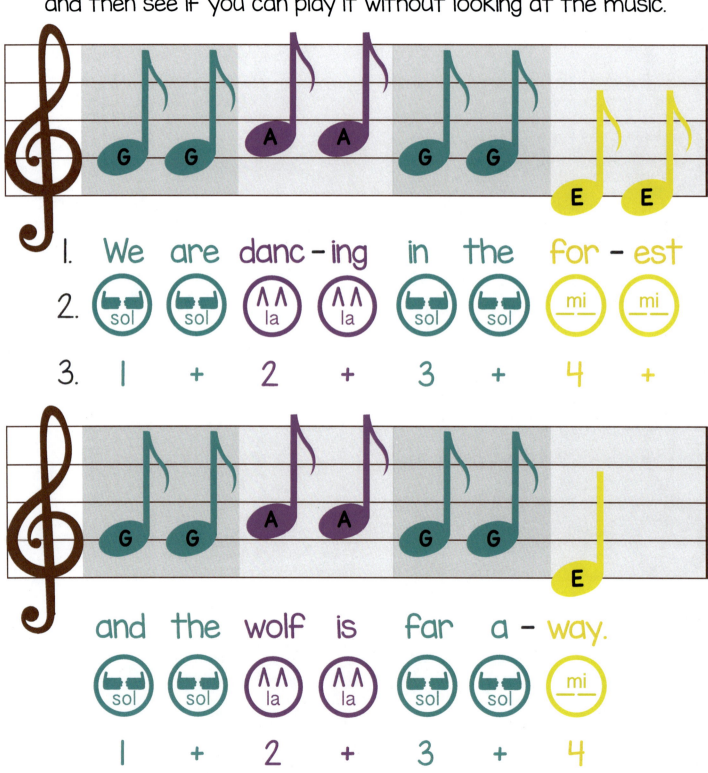

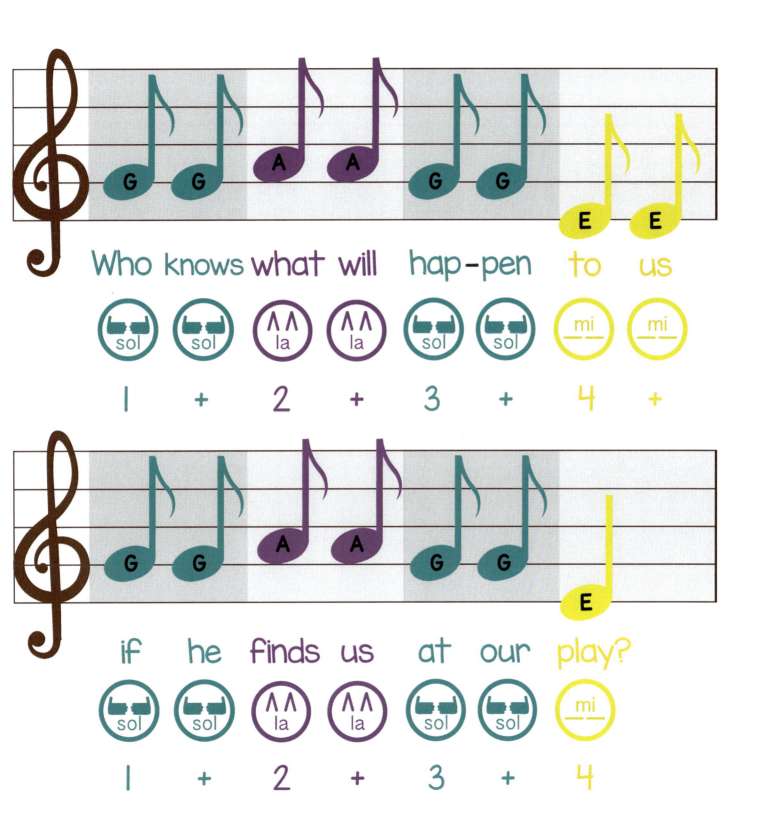

Wrong Note

Some of these notes are in the wrong place! Draw an X through them.
Hint: there are 10 wrong notes on the page!

Match the Numbers

Draw a line between each Solfège hand-sign and the correct number it represents.

Preschool Prodigies – Chapter Five Workbook

Hand-Sign Memory

Cut out each pair of hand-signs, flip them over, and play the classic game Memory! On each turn, a player flips two squares. If the squares match, that player collects those squares. The player with the most matches at the end of the game wins!

Preschool Prodigies - Chapter Five Workbook

Chapter 5 🎵 Section L: What Note Is It? 🎵 Lesson Guide

Objective
By the end of this section, students should be able to differentiate between E, G and A.

Overview
In this section, students identify the notes E, G and A by ear.

Essential Question
How can a student differentiate between the notes E, G and A?

Instruction Tips
If your students need additional practice, just have them record their answers on a separate piece of paper, or have them hold up the correct hand-sign to indicate their guess.

Materials
- What Note Is It? Video Access
- Workbook pages: 80

Table of Contents
What Note Is It?   80

Complementary Activities
Instead of students guessing along with the video, have them play E, G and A for each other and guess in pairs.

Section 5.L Video Annotations

0:27 Pause and make sure that each student has E, G and A out. Give them time to play each bell and say its note name.

0:46 Pause and let your learner guess the first note name before Rex reveals it!

1:10 Pause and let your learner guess the second note name before Rex reveals it!

1:34 Pause and let your learner guess the third note name before Rex reveals it! Explain to students that this will be the last time you pause before moving on. Be sure that your learner is circling his or her guesses on the What Note Is It workbook page.

Preschool Prodigies - Chapter Five Workbook

What Note Is It?
Draw a circle around the bell you hear in each box!

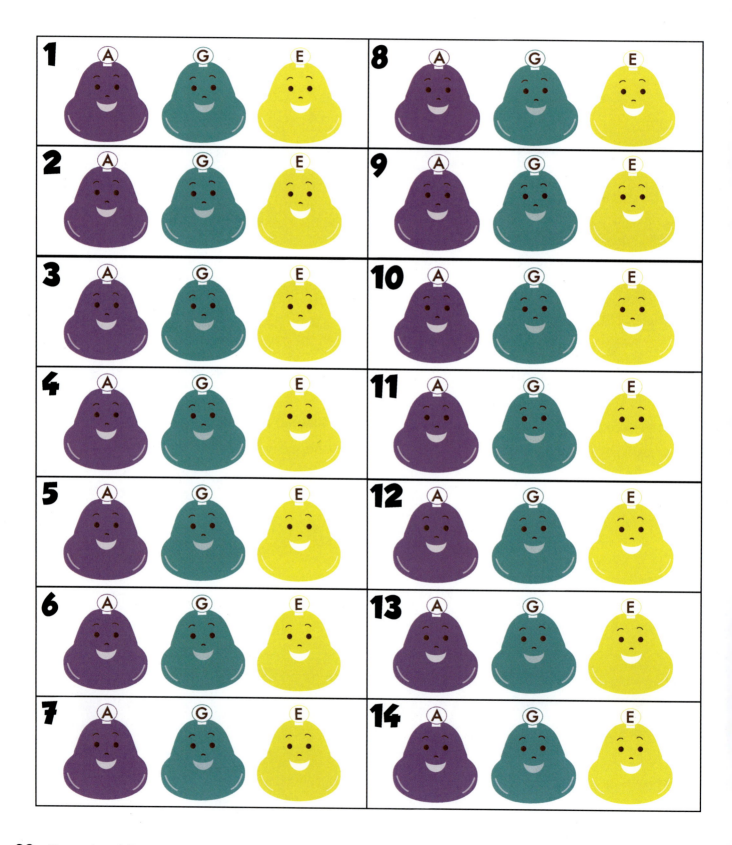

Prodigies Playground
CONGRATULATIONS

You've Completed

Preschool Prodigies
CHAPTER 5
Nice work!

_____ _____
Teacher Signature   Date

Preschool Prodigies – Chapter Five Workbook